Original title:
Sun-drenched Shores

Copyright © 2025 Creative Arts Management OÜ
All rights reserved.

Author: Zachary Prescott
ISBN HARDBACK: 978-1-80581-615-7
ISBN PAPERBACK: 978-1-80581-142-8
ISBN EBOOK: 978-1-80581-615-7

Morning's Warm Caress

The roosters crow, they sing with glee,
While I stumble out, still half asleep.
A tanuki wears my beach umbrella,
Is it a fashion choice or just a fella?

Waves crash loud, they laugh at me,
As I trip on sand, quite clumsily.
Seagulls steal my fries on a whim,
I'd save them, but my hopes are slim!

The sun climbs high, it's burning bright,
A lobster's glow, what a funny sight.
My skin turns red, oh such delight,
Next time I'll just stay inside tight!

Crabs dance the cha-cha, quick and spry,
While I sip soda, waving goodbye.
Beach days are wild with laughter and cheer,
I'll wear sunscreen next year, that's clear!

The Dreamy Dune Dance

On golden hills, my flip-flops fly,
I trip on the sand and nearly cry.
The palm trees sway, they tease and grin,
As I stumble near that mischievous fin.

I built a castle, oh what a sight,
Only for waves to claim it outright.
Sandy bricks, my throne now lost,
Just a seaweed crown, it's not worth the cost!

Seagulls hold court in a raucous line,
Squawking protests for my lunch divine.
As fries disappear, I can only pout,
They're plotting a coup, there's no doubt!

The day winds down, with toes in the sea,
Splashing and laughing, just pure glee.
When nightfall comes, the stars all prance,
Now it's time for the moonlit dance!

The Lure of Limelight

Beneath the bright umbrellas, we twirl,
My friend trips over a beach ball, what a whirl!
Seagulls steal our French fries in flight,
We chase them on sand, what a sight!

We build castles that wobble and sway,
Challenging waves to come out and play.
A crab waves back as it scuttles away,
While sunscreen meltdowns take turns in the fray.

Shoreline Serenade

On golden grains, we do our dance,
Spilling lemonade as we laugh, take a chance!
With every splash, we giggle with glee,
As my buddy insists he can swim like a bee.

A dolphin leaps, or maybe it's just a fish,
Ice cream drips down, how sweet is this wish?
We trip on flip-flops, but who even cares?
Just wave to the seagulls with crumbs in our hairs.

Whispering Zephyrs

The breeze whispers secrets as it tugs on my hat,
A sandcastle pirate tells me, 'I'm really a cat!'
Our floating raft joins a race with a shoe,
There's laughter galore, who knew it was true?

We spot a surfboard but it's really a plank,
An inflatable shark gives my buddy a prank.
With a splash and a squeal, we all disappear,
Emerging like mermaids with no trace of fear.

Where Ocean Kisses Sky

Dancing waves invite, I say 'bring it on',
Gulls deliver my sandwich, it's so far gone.
My toes get buried in a sand dune of fun,
I declare it's a treasure, a shiny baked bun.

The horizon glows with colors so bright,
As we fall over flippers, what a comical sight!
Laughter echoes as the sun starts to fade,
With footprints of joy, our memories are made.

Ocean's Embrace at High Tide

The waves come in, a playful tease,
They splash my toes, oh, what a breeze!
I dance away, like a fish on land,
While seagulls laugh, so close at hand.

Buckets tipped, my treasure spills,
Shells roll away, oh what a thrill!
I chase the tide, it rings my bell,
"Come back!" I shout, but it won't dwell.

Collecting Light Along the Coast

With buckets bright and nets held high,
We hunt for crabs beneath the sky.
One pinches hard, I let out a squeal,
"Hey there, buddy, let's make a deal!"

The sandcastles crumble, the tide rolls in,
We laugh at how we can't seem to win.
A seagull steals my tasty chip,
Guess it's a snack for a feathered dip!

Mellow Dunes and Gentle Rhymes

The dunes are soft, a playground grand,
I tumble down, oh, isn't it bland?
My friends all giggle, they point and tease,
"You look like seaweed!" as I sneeze.

With kites that soar and drift away,
We race them down, what a fine play!
But oh, that gust made one crash land,
"Return to me!" I holler, arms fanned.

Tidal Adventures Beneath Golden Skies

The fish are jumping, the kids all shout,
As I trip and fall, they laugh, no doubt!
I'm part of the sea now, a splashy sight,
Waves tease my nose, what a funny fright!

I try to surf, but I skim and slide,
While dolphins giggle, they cheer me wide.
One little wave gives a final prank,
And now I'm soaked, fresh from the tank!

Chasing the Horizon's Glow

Footprints race through grains of gold,
Seagulls squawk secrets, wild tales told.
A sandcastle army, ready to fight,
With shells for weapons, all day and night.

Flip-flops flying, they take to the air,
A splash of cold waves, without a care.
Where sunbeams tickle the tips of our toes,
We laugh at the tide, as it ebbs and flows.

Beachcomber's Reverie

Collecting odd treasures, a bottle's found,
Inside, a note: 'Just whistling around.'
A penguin in sunglasses, with sunblock on,
Says, 'Keep it cool, man, till the morning dawn!'

Flip-flops and flippers dance in the sand,
While jellyfish giggle, they form a band.
Crabs wearing vests strut in a line,
It's a beach party here, and we're feeling fine!

The Color of Afternoon Whispers

The sky spills lemonade, sweet on the shore,
As laughter bubbles, who could ask for more?
Kites in bright colors, they soar with glee,
While the wind plays tricks, just wait and see!

A barbecue's smoking, with burgers in sight,
But seagulls swoop down, oh what a delight!
One steals a bun, like a bandit at play,
And we're left with crumbs at the end of the day.

Daylight's Kiss on the Water

Waves tickle toes in a bubbly embrace,
While sunscreen rebels, becomes part of the race.
A dolphin does tricks, a playful ballet,
In flip-flops we cheer, as they steal the day!

A beach ball bursts forth, an explosion of cheer,
Rolling away, like it knows no fear.
With ice cream in hand, dripping down the cone,
We savor each moment, not wanting to moan.

Golden Waves Beckon

A seagull stole my sandwich, oh dear,
I chased it down, my lunch disappeared.
With salty air and sand stuck to toes,
I laughed as the tide tickled my nose.

The beach ball flew, another aimless toss,
Landed on a crab, who looked quite cross.
We played fetch until the sun sank low,
Now that's a game, I think I'll bestow.

Afternoon Light on the Sand

The sun is hot, my ice cream's in danger,
Melting fast, it's looking like a stranger.
I tried to catch it, what a sticky mess,
It dripped on my toes, I must confess.

The kids run wild, with laughter so bright,
One tripped on a flip-flop, what a sight!
Parents here with drinks, all sunk in sand,
Who needs a gym when nature's so grand?

Whispering Tides at Dusk

A crab just pinched my toe, oh what fun,
I waddle away, this crab's on the run.
The waves sing songs that make seaweed dance,
While I pretend I'm in a wave-washed trance.

Footprints trailing, in patterns so bizarre,
Like toddlers painted with muddy tar.
A splash to cool off, a wave's surprise,
Cold and retreating, with all laughing eyes.

Serenity Beneath Radiant Skies

Sunglasses on, but my nose turns red,
The sun's got jokes, it fills me with dread.
Beach towels out, we lay like fine cheese,
Nature's bistro, with movement to tease.

The sunset glows, like a melted crayon,
As beach games end, there's a new plan.
With laughter echoing, the day we'll recall,
Life's funny little moments, the best of them all.

Tide Pools in the Afternoon Glow

Little crabs in their fancy suits,
Dancing sideways in pursuit.
A starfish with a smile so wide,
Winks at shells that drift and glide.

Seagulls squawk, they think they're kings,
Swooping down for shiny things.
A beach ball goes for an unplanned flight,
As kids laugh loud under broad daylight.

Summer's Embrace at Water's Edge

Flip-flops fly, it's quite a scene,
While sunscreen is the unfavored cream.
Sandcastles rise with dubious grace,
As a rogue wave gives them a chase.

Hot dogs sizzle, what a treat,
But ketchup is spilled on the seat.
A frisbee lands in a nearby snack,
And a picnic is saved with a quick smack!

Castaway Comforts Under Open Skies

A cooler's singing, it's full of glee,
But the lid won't pop, oh woe is me!
From the back, a voice calls out,
'Let the ice cream fight begin, no doubt!'

Shady trees with gossiping leaves,
Watch out for ants, they're true thieves.
A hammock swings, but it's too tight,
Landing with a plop is quite the sight!

The Promise of Salt and Sun

Lemonade stands make a grand debut,
While kids giggle, claiming they're cool.
Seashells whisper secrets on the shore,
As waves clap hands for an encore.

In the distance, a buoy goes 'bleep',
While beach towels look like a mess heap.
Caught in laughter and sand's embrace,
Every dash returns without a trace!

A Palette of Warmth

A beach ball bounces high,
The seagulls dive, oh my!
Sandy toes in flip-flops
Giggling till the laughter stops.

Ice cream drips down the cone,
Melting fast, you moan and groan.
A towel wrapped like a cape,
Superheroes in the sun escape.

In the cooler, snacks collide,
Chips and soda side by side.
Picnic blankets flung with glee,
Bikini contests you can't unsee!

Sunburned noses all around,
Too much fun from ground to sound.
With laughter echoing bright,
Who needs sleep on such a night?

Beachcomber's Daydream

Waves that whisper secrets sweet,
Searching for shells, oh what a treat!
A crab in sandals takes a stroll,
Letting all the kids feel whole.

Frisbees flying way too far,
Landing on a lifeguard's car.
Sun hats spinning like a top,
Everyone's dancing, don't dare stop!

Sandcastles reach for the sky,
With moats that wonders satisfy.
Bucket brigade of tiny hands,
Creating dreams on golden sands.

A treasure map drawn in laughter,
A pirate finding joy thereafter.
Let's dig deep in sandy piles,
And make this beach life full of smiles!

Glimmers on the Water's Edge

Under the beach umbrella wide,
Napping while the waves collide.
A seagull steals your crunchy snack,
He knows just how to pick the pack.

Flip-flops flapping, now they run,
Chasing shadows, oh what fun!
Dolphins leap just out of sight,
Waving their tails, what a delight!

A beachcomber's hat flies away,
Off to join the seagull's play.
Tanning lotions start to blend,
Somehow, we all just pretend.

Splash fights start, laughter's grand,
Water splashes went as planned.
A sunset shows, a painting rare,
Who knew salty air could lead to flair?

Celestial Dusk

As day turns into magic night,
Bonfire circles glow so bright.
S'mores and stories, laughter rings,
Under stars, our joy takes wings.

Marshmallows dance on sticks so long,
Each bite shared feels like a song.
The moon peeks through the misty haze,
While shadows play in evening's gaze.

Twinkling lights in draping trees,
Breeze tickles and whispers, 'Do as you please!'
A dance party on the sand begins,
Barefoot steps, wild grins, no sins.

With waves that shimmer, curtains fall,
To a silent beach, we hear the call.
Laughter echoing through the night,
Who knew that wrong could feel so right?

Sunlit Currents

On sandy beaches, toes do wiggle,
Seagulls cackle, as they jiggle.
The waves come in with a silly splash,
While sunscreen thwarts the sun's warm clash.

Flip-flops dance, a rhythmic chatter,
Ice cream melts, guess that's the matter.
Children giggle, sandcastles tall,
A crab appears, and it's quite the brawl.

Beach umbrellas sway, like silly hats,
Funny hats spin, caught by the cats.
Tanned tourists strut, like peacocks proud,
With a knack for getting lost in the crowd.

As evening falls, the warmth persists,
With beach games played amid the twists.
We laugh as dusk brings a gentle nudge,
Life's better at the shore, we just won't judge!

The Quiet Roar of Warmth

The sun arises with a cheeky grin,
An ode to all the fun about to begin.
Beach balls bounce like happy folks,
While seagulls plot their breakfast jokes.

A giant sandworm takes its stroll,
With tiny shovels, we dig a hole.
The tide rolls in with a playful push,
As we chase it down in a happy rush.

Friends throw frisbees, oh what a sight!
One hits a stranger, oh what a fright!
Laughter echoes, the joy ignites,
While sunscreen fights its slippery rights.

As day fades out with a golden glow,
We dance on the shore, oh don't be slow!
With silly moves under twilight's bloom,
We find our groove, accounted for room!

Shoreline Whispers

Whispers of waves, a friendly tease,
As crabs throw sideways moves with ease.
Buckets and shovels scatter about,
While sunburnt dudes begin to pout.

Seashells giggle, as they're picked up,
Sandy toes wriggle in a big cup.
A sun hat flies off, like a bird so bold,
Chasing after it feels like a story told.

Sand angels made with an awkward flair,
You wish to see them, but you just can't share.
As waves crash down with a playful roar,
The tide decides, we'll never keep score.

We gather 'round for a toast of cheer,
With lemonade jammed, it's finally here.
Laughter erupts with each salty breeze,
Making memories with the utmost ease!

Glowing Tides

The tide rolls in with a goofy grin,
Splashing friends, where do I begin?
Finding shells, bringing giggles near,
While crabs offer their own kind of cheer.

A beach ball fights with a sudden gust,
Dodging everyone, it's a must.
Kids chase after, with a shout so loud,
Creating chaos, like a jokester crowd.

Sunburned noses are all around,
Slathered in lotion, we're tied and bound.
Snorkels clink as we dive for fun,
Emerging proud, like we've just won.

As twilight falls with a sparkling hue,
We'll dance and laugh, just us few.
With waves still rolling, bringing delight,
We treasure each moment, under starlight.

Secrets Beneath Shimmering Skies

On the beach, a crab wears a hat,
Proudly strutting, well, imagine that!
Seagulls squawk in a gossiping spree,
While a clam plays poker, just wait and see.

Sandcastles rise like silly towers,
Decorated proudly with candy flowers.
The tide comes in, a thief in the night,
Yet the mermaid just laughs, oh what a sight!

Under the waves, there's a dance they say,
With fish in tuxedos, they sway and display.
A dolphin does flips, not missing a beat,
While the octopus serves up a snack to eat.

Even the sun wears a pair of shades,
As beachgoers dive, forming fun parades.
Secrets are whispered in waves and foam,
Here on this shore, we all feel at home.

Where the Ocean Meets Daydreams

A starfish sings with a croaky voice,
To a sea turtle, who has no choice.
They claim that jellyfish are the stars,
Sailing their dreams in seaweed cars.

With beach balls bouncing, the laughter flies,
Coconuts roll like comical spies.
As waves do the cha-cha against the rocks,
Crabs in bow ties tap dance like flocks.

A message in a bottle, a hidden joke,
Written by the waves, or maybe a bloke.
Fish line up for a selfie, you see,
With a backdrop of bubbles, joyful and free.

The sunset is painted with splashes of cheer,
As kites in the sky play hide and seek here.
And right at dusk, the party won't cease,
With sandmen in suits, it's laughter and peace.

Tides of Sunlit Laughter

On the shoreline, a dog in a hat,
Chases his tail, oh what of that!
The sand feels warm, like cookies fresh-baked,
While gulls make plans for a heist, unshaked.

Shells tell stories of bickering fish,
One wants a show, the other a dish.
The waves giggle softly, a ticklish tease,
As children create a sandpile with ease.

Drifting on floats, the dreams don't drown,
As laughter erupts like sprinkles in town.
A whale with a bow tie joins in the fun,
Saying, "Isn't life grand? Let's splash and run!"

By the twilight, the fun only grows,
With shadows dancing, and laughter in throes.
The coast is alive, with stories unique,
As tides of joy brim where the sea and day seek.

An Ode to Coastal Serenity

Waves waltz gently, like they own the floor,
While crabs play cards on the soft sandy shore.
Seagulls pirouette, won't take no for an answer,
As beachgoers trip, with moves like a dancer.

The sun takes a peek, through a fluffy cloud,
As a kid in a bucket feels snazzy and proud.
Chasing their dreams as they dash and dive,
While seaweed wigs keep the laughter alive.

Starfish toast marshmallows, talking all night,
To a crab in pajamas, oh what a sight!
Fish in the moonlight gather to sing,
As mermaids take selfies, capturing spring.

The horizon blushes as day bids adieu,
But those on the beach know just what to do.
They dance in the moonlight, hearts full and free,
Creating new memories, where laughter will be.

Tides of Light

The beach ball's flying far and wide,
While seagulls swoop and glide.
A flip-flop tosses to the side,
My sunscreen's left—oh, what a ride!

We race to be the first in line,
For ice cream that we think is fine.
But melting drips now intertwine,
On our noses, what a sign!

A crab who thinks he owns the sand,
Dances chaotically, so unplanned.
He pinches toes in a grizzled stand,
While we laugh loud, not quite grand!

With laughter echoing 'round the bay,
We build a castle, come what may.
But waves crash in and take away,
Our sandy dreams—oh, what a play!

Sand Beneath our Feet

The sandman's here, he's chilling out,
With grains that make us laugh and shout.
But every step we take, no doubt,
Is like a workout we can't live without!

In shades of pink that clash so bright,
We stroll along, feeling light.
Yet one falls down, what a sight,
And rolls like a burrito, pure delight!

We spot a jellyfish, what a tease,
It flops right by with elegant ease.
But watch your toes, it's no time to freeze,
Or you'll dance like a chicken in the breeze!

With each wave comes a splashy cheer,
As friends all gather 'round so near.
The ocean sings its funny sneer,
And we just laugh until the night is here!

Luminous Coastlines

The sun is laughing bright, you see,
As coolers brim with drinks for free.
We spill our snacks with such glee,
    And seagulls join our jubilee!

Flip-flops flapping down the shore,
One gets tossed in a friendly war.
We giggle hard, who could ignore?
These silly moments, we adore!

The lighthouse winks—what a prank,
Its light a beacon, a shining flank.
A kite flies high with colors banked,
While we just sit and give a wink!

Our footprints dance along the tide,
With every splash, we slip and slide.
This beachy joy cannot be denied,
Where laughter's found, and worries hide!

Radiant Reflections

Mirrored waters, giggles abound,
With splashes heard all around.
The frisbee flies, but where's the sound?
Oh look, the dog has it, how profound!

A tan looks great until it peels,
Like loose wallpaper, it reveals.
We laugh so hard, the truth it heals,
In this bright place, you can't conceal!

A sunhat's lost amidst the fun,
And sunscreen fights have just begun.
We cartwheel on, our day's not done,
Till evening falls, we watch the run!

As twilight wraps the day in cheer,
We share our tales, the end draws near.
With sparkling waves and joy sincere,
These moments shared, we hold so dear!

A Gentle Caress on Sheltered Sands

Waves tickle toes, oh what a tease,
Sandcastles crumble with a gentle breeze.
Umbrellas tilt, caught in a skirmish,
While seagulls plot a snack ambush, how ambitious!

Buckets spill, filled with dreams of gold,
While sunscreen debates if it's too bold.
The beach ball bounces, what a delight,
As kids giggle, chasing with all their might.

Shells whisper secrets, but do they know?
The tide's in a hurry, ready to show.
A jellyfish jives, with no dance skill,
As we laugh and trip, it's all part of the thrill.

Crabs clomp around, in their little show,
With sideways moves, they steal the show.
Laughter erupts, like waves on the shore,
Here's to fun times, who could ask for more?

Where the Light Dances with the Sea

Fishermen's tales cast netted dreams,
While dolphins plot pranks, or so it seems.
Beach towels nap, with no one to guard,
As snacks disappear, life isn't so hard.

Kites swirl high, in the clammy air,
While small dogs bounce, without a care.
Sandy toes revolt, in a sandy strike,
As everyone promises, "Just one more hike!"

The lifeguard's whistle, a proud little tune,
As folks fumble for drinks, spilling too soon.
But laughter erupts with each little gaff,
As we toast to the fun, and we giggle and laugh.

Sun dips low, casting shadows awry,
As the sky blushes with a cotton candy sigh.
We'll dance in the waves, see who can splash,
Fun shines bright, no need to be brash!

Echoes of Laughter on Coastal Breezes

A splash and a dash, oh what a sight,
The sand feels warm, the mood feels bright.
Chasing seagulls, what a clever ploy,
While we cackle and giggle, pure joy.

Games of frisbee, fumbles abound,
While grumpy old crabs march all around.
The chairs lean back, naps quickly fade,
As ice cream melts, into squeals of mirth parade.

Children roll, a sandy embrace,
While surfboards wobble, testing their grace.
Fried dough and giggles, all around,
Each joke gets funnier, as laughter resounds.

As sunset arrives, a glorious show,
We toast with our drinks, a clink, a glow.
With echoes of laughter, forever we'll see,
These funny beach moments are just meant to be.

The Horizon's Warm Hug

Balloons fly high, as we set the scene,
With laughter and chatter, a vibrant routine.
The sunset spills colors, like art gone awry,
While beachgoers trip, always one guy shy.

Footprints blend closely, as games unfold,
Siblings squabble over treasures of gold.
A starfish waves, trying not to be shy,
As sand rolls in, making waves pass by.

Ice cream drips, it marks every smile,
As silly hats balance, let's keep it in style.
The laughter flows, like the tide on the shore,
Each moment a treasure, who could ask for more?

The horizon grins, with waves that they hum,
We dance in the sand, oh what fun, here we come!
We'll cherish these times, as memories hug,
The warm feel of laughter, forever a tug.

Moondust and Shells at Twilight

At twilight's glow, the crabs do prance,
With tiny steps, they start to dance.
A conch shell blew a tune so bold,
The seagulls joined, or so I'm told.

The sand is warm, it tickles toes,
And in a hat, a fish bestows.
A jellyfish, on a float, looks grand,
It waves to folks on the fine, soft sand.

Shells whisper secrets in the night,
Of mermaids who lost their shells in fright.
With every wave, the ocean grins,
While giggling crabs plot silly sins.

In moondust dreams, we laugh and play,
As starfish cheer, hip-hip-hooray!
Together we weave this goofy tale,
Where laughter sails, and none can fail.

The Rhythm of the Distant Surf

The dolphins dance to the surf's sweet tune,
While seagulls squawk, beneath the moon.
Each wave a note, a splashy song,
That makes even crabs want to sing along.

The sandcastles collapse with a little shove,
The tide gives chase, but can't take love.
An octopus plays peek-a-boo with glee,
While a beach ball rolls far, like a runaway bee.

Children giggle at the jelly spread,
"Is that your lunch?" one curious head.
But laughter swirls in the salty air,
As waves tickle toes without a care.

The rhythm twists, a playful dance,
As flip-flops float, in a sea romance.
With each new wave, we jump and twirl,
In this silly game, we all just whirl.

Kaleidoscope of Ocean Hues

A palette spills across the shore,
Bright fish parade and loudly roar.
"Look! A turtle in shades of green!"
"Have you seen a creature so rotund and keen?"

Coral sways like a funky dress,
Waving to the fish, quite a mess.
Every splash brings giggles galore,
As tide pools host a crustacean store.

With pinks and blues, the sea does strut,
While crabs in sunglasses say, "What's up?"
A clownfish swimming with silly flair,
Turns 'round to give a fishy stare.

In these colorful waters, we laugh and chase,
Every splash brings joy, a bubbly race.
A kaleidoscope beneath the sun's warm glow,
Where fish wear hats and seashells flow.

Trails of Light Across the Sea

The moonlight spills like butter on bread,
As dolphins skitter, "Get outta bed!"
With sparkling trails on waters so cool,
Who knew fish loved to play the fool?

Glistening paths where laughter thrives,
Where seaweed wiggles and silliness dives.
"Is that a wave?" the sand crabs say,
As they roll over in a gleeful display.

Lights twinkle like stars upon a dance,
Even starfish join, if given the chance.
With giggles and cheers, the sea comes alive,
As the pelicans swoop, ready to dive.

On these glimmering trails, we run and glide,
With every splash, a sense of pride.
Where every wave tells a comical tale,
Of friends and fun, where we all prevail.

Warmth Where the Land Meets the Tide

Footprints in the sand, a clumsy race,
Seagulls stealing snacks, oh what a face!
Kites tangled in hair, laughter in the breeze,
Chasing after crabs, with such silly ease.

Sunscreen on my nose, looking like a clown,
Fell into the waves, oh, I could drown!
Sandcastles collapsing, a magnificent fail,
Waves rolled in with giggles, a sopping trail.

Flip-flops flying off, in the splash and play,
Ice-cream melty hands, brightening the day.
Shells that hold secrets, whispers of the sea,
Finding joy in chaos, wild and fancy-free.

Jumping in the tide, as if I was a kid,
Belly flops and cannonballs, all laughter hid.
With salty hair and sunscreen blobs galore,
Who needs a royal bath? I'll take this shore!

A Symphony of Light and Water

Sunlight winks and dances, a shimmered tease,
While I elegantly trip, just trying to seize.
A splash from a flipper, my friend's grand show,
A duck dives by with a not-so-dapper bow.

Bubbles pop like secrets, spiraling high,
A beach ball soaring past, oh my, oh my!
Laughter floats like petals, in the salty air,
Crabs are judging me, with their sidelong stare.

The ice-cream truck is here, the race begins,
Sprinting down the shore, where nobody wins.
With sticky fingers and giggles galore,
Life's a grand circus, who could ask for more?

Twisting to the rhythm, of waves on the sand,
Dreams washed away, like castles unplanned.
But in all the frolic, there's a truth so bright,
Every splash and fall just adds to the light.

Reflections of a Glorious Day

Golden rays sparkling, a light-hearted tease,
Looking for the perfect spot, oh, such unease!
The towel's in a tangle, my beachwear's on wrong,
Every little mishap just adds to the song.

With a frisbee flying, it hits me on the head,
The laughter that follows, a chorus widespread.
Kids splash around me, a watery storm,
In the midst of it all, I redefine 'warm'.

Snacks left unattended, the seagulls descend,
A comedic buffet, their feathers they send.
Sunglasses misplaced, on top of my hat,
Here comes the tide! Oh no, what's up with that?

As the sun dips lower, painting skies of red,
We pack up the chaos, filled with crumbs, oh dread.
Each walk home a journey, of giggles and slips,
Let's do it again, with salty sea trips!

When the Sea Meets the Light

The tide rolls in with chatter, a bubbly affair,
I wade through the ripples, without a care.
Caught in a whirlpool, of laughter and fun,
Life just keeps spinning, no need to run.

Sunglasses misted over, the view's gone awry,
As I almost dive in, a definitive 'why?'
Seashells are treasures, I'll hold them just right,
Only to find crabs think they're diamonds bright.

Sand beneath my toes, tickles me so sweet,
Rolling in with waves, I find my own beat.
Where puddles become pools, and laughs never cease,
This goofy adventure, surely brings peace.

As day meets the night, with stars twinkling bright,
The ocean tells tales, of joy and delight.
Let's toast with our sodas, and laugh till we tire,
In this hilarious haven, we never expire!

Golden Moments at the Water's Edge

Seagulls squawk, they steal my fries,
A sandy beach, where laughter flies.
The kid's bright bucket holds a shell,
But in it, a jellyfish does dwell!

A dog that chases its own tail,
Dives in the waves, it's quite the fail.
A frisbee zooms, it takes a dip,
Lands on a sunbather's sunblock strip!

Flip-flops clash in a vibrant dance,
While someone fumbles with their pants.
As sunscreen flies and giggles blend,
These golden moments never end!

With ice cream cones and sticky hands,
We build our castles, make our plans.
A wave attacks our fortress grand,
And we all just laugh, not quite as planned.

Golden Horizons

Colors splash as sunsets bloom,
A beach ball lands, a grand kaboom!
In the distance, kids race and cheer,
While ice cream drips and brings a jeer.

Umbrellas pop like mushrooms spry,
One flies away with a frantic sigh.
On the shore, a crab steals a crunch,
While we all gather for a munch.

Someone slips in a wave's embrace,
And drenches a friend, what a silly chase!
But laughs echo through the setting day,
As laughter leads us on our way.

With each wave that breaks on the sand,
We sketch our dreams with sticky hands.
The horizon glows, our hearts, they sing,
It's those funny moments, life's sweet fling!

Whispering Waves

Whispers rise from bubbles popped,
Where flip-flops flop, our laughter's dropped.
A picnic spread, a fine buffet,
Until the ants all join the play!

Waves hush secrets upon the shore,
As someone's hat goes for a soar.
And friends all laugh as it swims away,
While beach balls bumble in sunlit play.

A seagull eyeing a crusty chip,
Dares to swoop, oh, what a trip!
While sandcastles crumble, met with fate,
We all agree it's hard to hate!

With gentle tides and sun's soft glow,
Our funny tales keep on the flow.
When twilight wraps the day in grace,
We'll share our bloopers, time can't erase.

The Warm Embrace of Dawn

Morning breaks with colors bright,
As we all scramble in delight.
A coffee spill, it can't be tamed,
But laughter's spark can't be disclaimed!

With beach towels flying all around,
Our flip-flops dance as we hit the ground.
The ocean's tune calls out our names,
While dolphins play their silly games.

Someone's hat begins to sail,
Chased by winds, it's quite the trail.
A crab decides to join the fun,
Dancing sideways, oh, what a run!

As day unfolds, we giggle and sway,
Capturing moments without delay.
In the warm embrace of dawn's first light,
Our quirky memories take to flight.

A Symphony of Light

The seagulls dance, a joyful sight,
Their squawks compose a laugh at night.
Sandcastles rise, with dreams so grand,
But then they tumble, thanks to a hand!

The beach ball bounces, a rogue's delight,
It flies too far, oh what a flight!
Children chase it with giggles and glee,
Just don't let it land in the sea!

Ice cream drips down a sticky cone,
While sun hats dance like they're on loan.
Flip-flops flop, a rhythmic sound,
As laughter echoes all around.

And just when you think a crab will scurry,
It stops to dance, no need to hurry.
With a twist and a turn, it steals the show,
Who knew that crabs could put on a glow?

Sunlit Silhouettes

On the shore, shadows come to play,
Making shapes that dance and sway.
A dog runs past with a joyful bark,
Straight into the water, it leaves a mark!

Beach towels flutter like flags in the breeze,
While sunscreen fights to keep off the freeze.
A family picnic turns into a race,
As seagulls swoop down with hopeful grace.

Children laugh in a splish-splash spree,
Water balloons fly, oh, can't you see?
The waves join in, a bubbly embrace,
Their laughter mixing with this wild race!

While shells and treasures hide in the sand,
One's just a flip-flop—not what you planned!
But here we are, under skies so blue,
Creating memories the whole day through.

Waves of Warm Embraces

Crashing waves in a goofy fight,
Socks and sandals, what a sight!
Laughter spills as a splash takes aim,
And someone yells, 'Not again, my fame!'

The snacks are swiped by daring seagulls,
Who knew they could be such little fools?
Sandwiches fly like frisbees set free,
Just another wave of beach jubilee!

Sun hats twirl as they tumble around,
Someone dives in, and the waves resound.
Goggles slip down from a childish cheer,
As splashes proclaim, it's the best time of year!

The shoreline's alive with raucous delight,
Shorts and t-shirts take off in flight.
With each silly splash, joy finds its way,
As laughter and smiles rule the day!

The Golden Hour's Coast

Golden hues shine as the day ends,
Swimming suits change to quick-witted friends.
The beach bonfire crackles and pops,
As we roast marshmallows and swap funny flops!

Someone attempts to play the guitar,
But the tunes sound more like a wild car.
With every strum, a chuckle shared,
As jellyfish float, all poorly flared!

Sticky fingers clutch s'mores, oh my!
Chocolate and laughter make spirits high.
Flickers of light from the fire's spark,
As shadows dance like they're in the park!

So here we sit, under skies so bright,
Crafting tales that stretch into the night.
With waves as our audience, we'll float away,
In a sea of joy, we'll forever stay!

Glistening Shores of Memory

Memories dance on the sandy spree,
As seagulls squawk with curious glee,
Buckets and shovels, a castle so grand,
But soon it collapses, just like my plans.

Flip-flops a-flying, oh what a sight,
Chasing the waves, in pure delight,
Ice cream drips down, a sticky fate,
I thought I'd look cool—now I'm second-rate.

Friends take a plunge, but I must confess,
My splash is a flop, oh what a mess!
Laughter rings out, the tide takes my shoe,
Guess I'll be walking home barefoot, who knew?

With laughter and warmth, the days float away,
On this coastline where silliness plays,
I'll cherish these dodges from life's little stress,
A life full of joy—who needs more, I guess?

Barefoot Bliss on Coastal Trails

Wandering barefoot, oh what a thrill,
Sand between toes, now that's a skill,
Dodging the crabs with their tiny parade,
While I trip over shells—an odd masquerade.

Salty hair flops, oh fashion divine,
Forget the runway; this look's so fine,
Caught in a net of my own beach ball,
Beach volleyball? More like a fumble and fall!

The tides rise up like a dance-off surprise,
Splashing my friends, oh my, what a prize!
Chasing the surf, with giggles and cheer,
Forgot my sunscreen—ouch, now I revere!

With laughter that echoes, the day fades away,
These barefoot adventures—a grand cabaret,
Next time I'll wear shoes, or will I just dare?
Who needs 'em anyway? I'll let down my hair!

Golden Hour's Tender Touch

As the light dips low, oh what a scene,
Golden hues wrapping like ice cream,
Sandcastles glimmer with sunset's embrace,
A perfect place to just make a face.

Crabs take the stage, with a wibbly walk,
Stealing my spotlight; oh, what a shock!
Smirking at sunsets while munching on snacks,
Life's grand stage where laughter never lacks.

Friends spin around, trying to catch,
Fleeting sea breezes—what a mad match!
And just in the season with nothing to lose,
Except my own dignity—I'll pay my dues!

As colors fade out and stars take their turn,
I wish for the laughter and all that I learn,
In these golden moments where silliness sows,
A garden of memories where friendship still grows.

Turquoise Dreams in Luminous Waves

Diving in turquoise, where laughter ignites,
Flipping and flopping like seals on delights,
Waves give a push, or a comical toss,
I tumble and splatter like a well-sauced boss.

Floating on floaties, feeling so free,
Sunscreen applied—no chance for a spree,
But whoops! I forgot the back of my neck,
A lobster, I'm not; more like a trainwreck!

With splashes and giggles, we ride the big curls,
Splashing our friends is just one of our twirls,
A shark might appear! Oh no, it's just Joe,
Living his best life with his beach ball to show.

The day winds down under skies painted bright,
With memories crafted in sheer pure delight,
So raise a glass high, here's a toast to our flops,
In shimmering waters, where laughter never stops!

Coastal Whispers of Forgotten Tales

The seagulls squawk their secret strain,
While sandcastles melt, like dreams in rain.
A crab wearing sunglasses, so out of place,
Dances with jellyfish in a clumsy race.

A floatie dog claims his reign of the beach,
His splashes draw laughter, the waves they beseech.
With shades on his nose, he barks at the tide,
While toddlers build towers, with giggling pride.

Old fishermen swap all their tales and winks,
Their faces as crinkled as worn-out sphinxes.
"Caught a big one!" They boast, with eyes all aglow,
While their bait is just chips from a nearby taco.

A sunhat-wearing cat, lounging free,
Snores through the chaos, as happy as can be.
The hidden life here, both humorous and grand,
Whispers us tales from this whimsical land.

Beneath the Glint of Endless Blue

A fish in a bowtie swims by with a grin,
Waving hello to the beach bumkin kin.
While dolphins in tuxedos perform their cool tricks,
And surfers collide as they tumble like bricks.

Umbrella drinks spill in a colorful mess,
While sunburned tourists claim they're well-dressed.
A flip-flop brigade takes charge of the shore,
Chasing after beach balls, oh, what a chore!

Sand made of sugar seems tempting to eat,
While ants hold a party beneath our sore feet.
Somewhere a man juggles, with style and flair,
But drops all his oranges, much to our despair.

Night falls in colors of orange and pink,
While beachgoers dance as they munch on a stink.
With laughter afloat, these moments we cherish,
As silly sights linger long after they perish.

Heartbeats in the Sand

Footprints tell stories of countless feet,
As frisbees soar high, and kids squeal in heat.
A turtle on a journey, oh so very slow,
Choices of a sunburned child, where will he go?

Beach chairs unite in the ultimate war,
As sunscreen shenanigans stick to the floor.
Splashing our neighbors as high tides roll in,
Creating a ruckus, oh, brother, we win!

A parrot named Polly, with a colorful tale,
Mocks the lifeguard's whistle and will never fail.
While beach bums laze, sipping drinks from a cup,
The waves keep on crashing, with laughter mixed up.

Sand angels repose on this sandy white bed,
Spreading forgetfulness over our sleepy heads.
As night draws a curtain, and lanterns ignite,
We giggle and whisper at the summer delight.

Mirage of Sunlit Delight

A mirage appears, is it a ship or a dream?
While surfers conspire in their sun-kissed scheme.
Pink flamingos wiggle, they rule the parade,
Strutting their stuff, though slightly afraid.

A sandworm in shades, oh, what a sight!
Doing the cha-cha, under the moonlight.
Beachcombers scatter, a collective search,
For seashells that fit with their colorful merch.

Somehow a beach ball gets stuck in a tree,
While a child yells, "Mom, it's drowning at sea!"
A sandman weaves tales with his infinite grace,
While sunscreen saves each rosy little face.

Under the stars, the antics unwind,
Floating away as if life's all designed.
With giggles and cheers, the night carries on,
In the laughter of waves, we find our sweet song.

A Palette of Memories at Sea

A crab in a hat tries to dance,
While seagulls squawk as if in a trance.
With sunscreen blobbed on all the wrong spots,
We're laughing so hard, all are tied in knots.

The waves tickle toes as they rush and roll,
A fish flips by, playing the sole,
Our dog steals a sandwich, a sneaky heist,
His guilty look brings laughter to feast.

The sky is a canvas where kites take flight,
We race with the breeze, all feeling so light.
With bucket and spade, we build a grand tower,
Until it's a puddle! What a grand hour!

Then a seagull drops in, thinks he's a guest,
He steals our fries, is he not impressed?
We wave our arms, it's a comic parade,
Our luck with the beach food? Oh dear, it's played!

Gentle Lapping on Time-Worn Shores

The tide rolls in with a giggly tease,
Footprints washed away with such lack of ease.
A kid throws a tantrum, the bucket's not fair,
While mom builds a castle with sand in her hair.

A dolphin leaps with a wink and a swirl,
As we try to dodge the curve of a twirl.
In flip-flops so floppy, we wobble and sway,
An unexpected splash steals our breath away!

The sun wears a crown of cotton candy fluff,
We ponder our ice cream—oh, where's the scoff?
When all turns chaotic, the ice cream slips low,
A dog sits and watches, all slack in a row.

We pack for the day; our towels all cling,
There's much to remember, our hearts start to sing.
With laughter like bubbles that float in the air,
We leave the shore, but our joy lingers there.

Enchanted Moments Under Bright Canopies

Beneath big umbrellas, we laugh at our fate,
Our snacks turn to sand, oh isn't that great?
Sipping on juice boxes like bold little champs,
While ants plan an invasion; how brave are those stamps?

A kite gets tangled with someone's hat,
We giggle aloud to see where it's at.
Someone's caught sunburn—oh, what a delight,
Red as a lobster, they're quite the sight!

The beach ball rolls free, it has its own will,
As we chase it down, what an ultimate thrill!
Sunscreen applies like a jelly-like mess,
We give out high fives, our mark of success.

The tunes in the air get us all on our feet,
Dance like no one's watching; oh isn't that sweet?
With laughter and joy that won't ever cease,
We treasure these moments—a heart's perfect piece.

Essence of Warmth and Water

The waves whisper secrets as they crash and sway,
While kids yell with glee, 'We're surfing today!'
Mom's hair is a nest, her style takes a break,
A crab scurries by, we can't help but shake.

Ice cream cones wobble like towers of dreams,
With drips and with giggles, we dare to extremes.
A flip in some sand turns to evidence bold,
Why take just one scoop when it can be sold?

The sun dips low, painting skies orange and pink,
As we float in our thoughts, we're right on the brink.
A beach ball deflates, but spirits stay bright,
We'll cherish this madness, our hearts take flight.

With towels as capes, we roam like it's fate,
The sand in our shoes, oh must we debate?
We head home, all sandy, a colorful trace,
These moments we treasure, the smiles we embrace.

Nature's Ballet of Light and Wave

The seagulls throw a party, loud and shrill,
While crabs do the conga, up and down the hill.
A beach ball bounces by, it's a wild chase,
And every wave comes in with a funny face.

Flip-flops splapping, dancing on the sand,
While kids are making castles, isn't life just grand?
A sun hat flies off, oh what a sight,
It lands on a dolphin, making quite the flight!

Sunscreen fights break out, it's a slippery game,
While someone yells, "Help, I'm stuck like a flame!"
The tide steals the snack, right out of my hand,
But laughter rolls in just like the sand.

Even the sun seems to giggle a bit,
As umbrellas tumble, making a quick exit.
Nature's a comedian, don't you agree?
Laughter and waves, so wild and free!

Eternal Summer at Water's Edge

On golden grains, we frolic and run,
The ice cream melts fast, oh what a fun!
Parents chase toddlers, it's a wild scene,
While dogs strategize, "I'll be the king!"

With a splash and a giggle, the fun is contagious,
And every misstep feels rather outrageous.
The tide takes a shoe, oh what a delight,
Did it swim off? This gives us a fright!

Popsicles drip, leaving a sweet trace,
While sandcastles crumble; it's a sad race.
The seagulls squawk loudly, plotting a heist,
To steal those fries—oh, they're so nicely spiced!

As dusk paints the waves in a glittery spray,
We wave to the sun, kinda hoping it'll stay.
But soon it will set, let out a sigh,
"Don't worry, I'll be back, oh my, oh my!"

The Lure of Horizon's Glow

The horizon glitters, a treasure chest bold,
While beachgoers search for sea glass and gold.
Each wave brings a giggle, a splash makes us scream,
As laughter erupts like it's all a big dream.

A kite takes flight, dancing high in the sky,
While kids shout, "Look! There's a fish swimming by!"
With flip-flops outsmarting each footstep we take,
The sand's like quicksand, a tricky mistake!

A sunscreen mishap, covered head to toe,
The laughter ignites like a fun-loving show.
Seagulls hover close, with their quest for a snack,
While we cheer them on, "Give that chip back!"

The breeze tells a tale of joy and delight,
As flip-flops go flying, oh what a sight!
The day wraps up snug in a warm pastel glow,
With memories made, it's a comedic show!

Dancing Shadows on the Beach

Shadows skitter and scamper, oh what a sight,
Dancing like socks in a washing machine fight.
With each wave's retreat, a footprint appears,
Erased by the tide, it brings laughter and cheers.

Oops! There goes a frisbee, spinning in glee,
While a dog claims it boldly, invigorated and free.
The laughter is contagious, a summertime call,
While balance is lost, we're ready to fall.

Tickling toes in the surf, how can it be?
The water's made of giggles; it's an ocean spree!
Someone's hat now floats off, waving hello,
While the wind plays its tricks in a flamboyant show.

Sunset drapes the beach in a legacy bright,
As shadows play tag under the fading light.
It's a carnival of moments, a twist of fate,
On this lively seashore, we incessantly wait!

Tangled Dreams in Sunlit Rays

On a beach towel, my snacks have fled,
Seagulls plot with mischief, I'm misled.
I chase my chips, they swoop and soar,
Laughter echoes, I'll buy snacks galore!

Flip-flops flop as I run for my fries,
Dancing in circles under clear blue skies.
My hat flies off, wild winds have their fun,
This beachside circus has only begun!

Budgies peek at my soda-brimmed crown,
As I splash in waves, they chase me down.
With salty hair and stories to share,
Tomorrow, I'll aim for a seabird's lair!

Time flies fast, a tumble then a spill,
Covered in sand, I'm getting my fill.
With every trip, I laugh 'til I cry,
This tangled bliss, oh my, oh my!

Where Water Meets Golden Sand

Kites rise high with a cheeky twist,
They dive and swoop, I can't resist.
I grab my drink, but it's full of sea,
That's what I get for being so free!

My friend builds castles, towers so grand,
While I construct a moat, oh so bland.
A wave comes crashing, his fortress is gone,
Laughter erupts at this watery con!

We play beach volleyball until we tire,
The ball flies off, and sparks a new fire.
Chasing it down, I stumble and fall,
Muffled giggles behind me, I hear them all!

As the tide rolls in, our day winds down,
Covered in sand, like a beach-bound clown.
With selfies snapped, we pose and we grin,
This sandy saga, let the good times begin!

Embracing the Day's Last Light

With a drink in hand, the sky turns gold,
I trip on my towel, yet I'm bold!
The horizon chuckles, the water glows,
As I take a seat right in a row!

Swaying to tunes, I try to dance,
But the sand holds tight, no room for chance.
The sun waves goodbye with a mischievous wink,
Should I leap or just have one more drink?

Footprints behind, as I sprint on the shore,
The sunset giggles, but I want more.
I juggle my snacks while I hop on one foot,
As the world around me starts to boot!

That's when I see, my flip-flop's a goner,
Floating away like a lazy wanna-be loner.
But the sun just blushes, dips low for a cheer,
As I dive for my shoe with no hint of fear!

Reflections on Shimmering Water

Mirrored waves reflect my silly pose,
With one flailing arm, and the other—who knows?
I slip in the foam, make quite the splash,
The fish stare back, "Is that an odd flash?"

I float on my back with a gleeful grin,
But seagulls decide it's their turn to spin.
They dance around, dropping seaweed confetti,
I laugh at the antics, it's far from petty!

Noodles and chips make quite the mess,
As tides twist and twirl in a playful caress.
Caught in the ebb, I might just stay,
Pretending that this is my kind of play!

The sun starts to yawn, its day's work is done,
As I splash in the tide, oh what fun!
With giggles and glee, let's make a toast,
To shimmery waters and laughing the most!

Laughter Echoes on Warm Breezes

The sand ticks my toes, oh what a tease,
My hat flies away, caught up in the breeze.
A seagull squawks loud, like it owns the place,
I chase it in vain, what a comical race.

A child builds a castle, right next to mine,
His moat is a puddle—oh how it does shine!
I splash with delight, water flies in the air,
We giggle so hard, throwing worries to care.

An ice cream truck drives, I leap with a cheer,
Only to trip on my flip-flops right here.
The world seems so funny, under bright, blissful rays,
All woes washed away, in these laughter-filled days.

So here's to the fun, on this beachy retreat,
With sand in my sandwich, and sun on my feet.
I'm ready to roll, in the waves and the sun,
With a heart full of laughter, we're all having fun!

A Dance of Light and Sea

The jellyfish waltz and the crabs do the crawl,
Shells wear tiny hats, oh aren't they so tall?
The splashes are music, a symphonic delight,
A dolphin joins in, puts on quite a sight.

I try to impress with my best belly flop,
But instead I just sink, oh will I ever stop?
The waves keep on laughing, they throw me about,
I emerge with a splash, feeling silly, no doubt.

A beach ball's my partner, we dance and we sway,
While sunscreen turns friends into human soufflés.
With shouts of pure joy and a few playful lies,
The sun grins down wide, as the day quickly flies.

So here on this canvas of blue and bright gold,
We paint silly moments, the laughter unfolds.
And as nighttime beckons, stars flicker and beam,
We waltz with the memories, in sweet, sandy dreams.

Radiant Horizons Call

The horizon's so bright, like a cheeky grin,
While I search for my sunglasses, where did I begin?
The tide crashes in, with its bubbly delight,
And I swear that it giggles when I run out of sight.

My towel's a ship, sailing out to the sea,
But the wind has a plan—it's a pirate with glee!
It yanks at my nap, as I drift into dreams,
A mermaid's sweet laughter bursts at the seams.

I attempt to build towers, but they all fall down,
While a crab in a tux gives me quite the frown.
He raises a claw as if making a speech,
Declaring my castle's not fit for the beach.

With footprints a mess and my hair full of sand,
We dance to the sunset, it's all unplanned.
Every crash of the waves, every laugh that we share,
Are treasures we gather from this shoreline affair.

Footprints in the Warm Embrace

Footprints that lead to mischief and fun,
My toes in the water, the day's just begun.
A splash to the left, and I slip to the right,
With everyone laughing at my new dance flight.

A pail full of dreams, I build up to the sky,
Then a wave steals my treasure, oh me oh my!
The tide's got a giggle, it swirls all around,
As I dive to recover, splash down without sound.

The sun starts to set, painting stories in gold,
While I spot a cool crab trying to break the mold.
He struts with style, a real beachside cat,
You've never seen swagger quite like that!

So here's to the laughter, the joy and the play,
The footprints we leave, all washed clean by the spray.
As the stars twinkle on, the surf gently sighs,
We'll dance through the night, where the fun never dies!

www.ingramcontent.com/pod-product-compliance
Lightning Source LLC
Chambersburg PA
CBHW072131070526
44585CB00016B/1624